ISBN 978-1-331-55405-9
PIBN 10205143

English
Français
Deutsche
Italiano
Español
Português

www.forgottenbooks.com

Mythology Photography **Fiction**
Fishing Christianity **Art** Cooking
Essays Buddhism Freemasonry
Medicine **Biology** Music **Ancient
Egypt** Evolution Carpentry Physics
Dance Geology **Mathematics** Fitness
Shakespeare **Folklore** Yoga Marketing
Confidence Immortality Biographies
Poetry **Psychology** Witchcraft
Electronics Chemistry History **Law**
Accounting **Philosophy** Anthropology
Alchemy Drama Quantum Mechanics
Atheism Sexual Health **Ancient History**
Entrepreneurship Languages Sport
Paleontology Needlework Islam
Metaphysics Investment Archaeology
Parenting Statistics Criminology
Motivational

FALLING
LEAVES

SARA A. C. PLUMMER

The writer of these desultory pages has no illusions concerning them. There is nothing to interest the general public; but if their compilation will please her own immediate family, and that small but very precious circle of personal friends who love her, the result will abundantly compensate the author.

SARA A. C. PLUMMER.

FALLING LEAVES

To A. W. C. in 1875

I remember what you said
When the stars shone overhead—
Frosty stars that gleamed above
When I saw you last, my love.

Hand in hand I said goodby;
Heart to heart you made reply—
"Footsteps parting in the snow
Meet again when roses blow."

Roses budded, bloomed and fled,
All the summer flowers are dead;
Autumn showered her rainy tears
Hopes are faded into fears.

Frosty stars are shining now
Once again above my brow—
Summer streams to ice are chilled
And thy promise unfulfilled.

Thinking of Memorial Day   1894

Millions of raindrops are falling today
Over the brown, thirsty breast of the earth;
Healing its barrenness—bringing to birth
The buddings of April, the blossoms of May.

Millions of grassblades are springing today
To cover the tokens of death and of blight—
They cover the graves of our dead from our sight;
So daintily thatching their mansions of clay.

Millions of teardrops are falling unheard—
Shed in humanity's uttermost need—
Save by the Healer—whose benefits speed
Who speaks to the nations with help in His word.

Millions of blood drops have fallen—Oh, God!
Treasure such showers in thy merciful Hand—
That travail-won harvests bloom rich in our land
As buddings and blossoms spring up from the sod!

Third M. V. I.   1884

The troubled peace at length was broke,
From lip to lip the tidings ran—
When rebel guns at Sumpter woke
The listening airs of Michigan.

Roused by the Nation's call to arms
The long roll beat from sea to sea;
From cities, villages and farms
Swept in the legions of the free.

A thousand rifles to the front,
A thousand boys in union blue—
They bring to stem the battle's brunt
A thousand patriot hearts and true.
    *   *   *   *   *   *

We saw them when they pressed before
The bravest in the army's van,
We knew when red Virginia's shore
Was wet with blood of Michigan.

We followed where the "Diamond" led
Victorious legions in the fight—
We heard brave Kearney when he said—
"Put Michigan on guard tonight."

We listened to their bugle's call—
We wept their fallen—but we knew
That He who marks the sparrow's fall
Could keep them, too.

High were their hopes, and high attained—
For glory hovered where they trod—
And he who brightest laurels gained
Received his honors from his God.

We greet them victors over wrong—
We hail them conquerers by right!
We strike the harp and weave the song
In valor's praise tonight.
      * . *   *   *   *   *

Oh, proud Peninsula! thro these—
For thee the blood of heroes runs;
Encircled by thine inland seas,
Thy noblest products are thy sons.

Fourth M. V. I.   1887

Are these the heroes of that day?
*   *   *   *   *   *
So light of step, so blithe were they—
Unclouded eyes and sun-bright hair—
Strong hearts where kindliness held sway,
Smooth cheeks and lips, and with an air
About each youthful, blue-clad form,
Of mother's clasp and kiss yet warm.

The loyal homes between the lakes
Held lonely hearts in Michigan;
They wore brave faces for your sakes,
Your bugle notes blew strong and free;
But their lone prayers rose silently,
Their hearts kept time with quickened beat
To the cadence of your marching feet.
*   *   *   *   *   *
Shine summer's sun! Again ye shine
As on that day at Gettysburg,
When loyal lives upon the shrine
Of Freedom's altar yielded free—
Where loyal blood was poured like wine
For God and sweet humanity.

We sing the praises of the boys
Who died for us mid smoke and flame,
Where trenches held them; or the claim
Of prison walls their bodies bound;
But whose freed spirits at the sound
Of God's voice upward sprang. They wait
To greet us at the Jasper gate.
Their sweet lives do not die unsung;
Age shall not touch them in its sway,
Forever beautiful and young,
We keep them in our hearts today!

Extracts from War Poems

Had you a lover in the ranks?
"Nay, then," she cried, "not one but two—
Swifter than eagles—stronger—finer
Than princes in their suits of blue.
And leaped my heart with joy and pride
To see them march beside the others;
With love—hope—dread—a mingled tide—
Because they were my soldier brothers."

The Tennessee Girl

The time was eighteen sixty-three,
When treason flaunted the rebel rag—
And loyal old East Tennessee
Lived two long years without the flag.

Years of sadness, of want, of fears—
Of exiled brothers and rifled home—
Years of longing, thro' strife and tears
To see the blue-clad army come.

How we welcomed them! Burnside's best!
Veteran heroes "grim and solemn—
Men from the grand old North and West"
Marched in many a line and column.

O, the joy of their bugle song!
O, the blissful beat of the drums!
When skirting the mountain sides along
The liberating army comes.

A Michigan regiment passed close by
Just there by that pine tree's lengthening shade,
And one of them carried—swung free and high—
A miniature flag on his bayonet blade.

    The dear old flag!

The tears leaped into my eyes like rain
"Hurrah for the Stars and Stripes!" I cried;
"I could kiss that soldier who brings again
The flag so long to our sight denied."

He heard me and came from the ranks with a smile,
"Your chance is good," were the words he said—
He leaned towards me over the stile
And I kissed his cheek—while my own flashed red.

But cheer on cheer went up from the troops,
Caps were lifted and tossed in play,
And the colonel said to the halting groups,
"I'll carry that flag the rest of the way."

Bronzed and brown was the boy I kissed,
He was a youth to love and sigh for
As he marched away thro the dusty mist,
A man to live for—a man to die for!

I watched that tossing flag on high
Till the faded Stars and Stripes grew dim
And I knew ere the rearmost ranks passed by
He had carried my heart away with him.

And if he fell in the cruel strife
And sleeps this blood-bought soil below,
If rendered up was the bright young life
In his country's cause—I shall never know.

Perhaps he lives: On a northern farm
I see him, sometimes, in my dreams:
A blue-eyed wife is on his arm,
The yellow harvest round him teems.

But in his deep eyes' tender gray
There lives no memory of me—
Who kissed him on that August day—
Under the pines of Tennessee!

The incident alluded to in the "Tennessee Girl" actually occurred when the Twenty-third Michigan Infantry, Second Brigade, Second Division, Twenty-third Army Corps marched with Burnside to rescue that portion of the State of Tennessee from the Rebels.

The soldier in the poem was the writer's brother—Samuel Cochrane, of Company "A."

The poem was written at Perry, Michigan, about 1886, and read the same day as part of the program of a Twenty-third Michigan regimental reunion. Nearly all of the original officers were present, as well as both brothers of the writer, Samuel Cochrane and Lieut. Isaac N. Cochrane. The. latter was the well-known physician and surgeon of Delphi, Indiana, where he settled after his graduation from the University of Michigan in 1868.

U. S. Grant

In the great Nation's greatest need we prayed
For succor: "God of Freedom, interpose,
And send a chosen man unto our aid."
This kingly warrior to our help arose
And beat to dust our foes.

A threshing instrument, divinely made
To put the slaveholder's rebellion down,
At his victorious feet our wreaths we laid,
And when we proffered more than kingly crown
To him, the world bowed down.

Ah, what avails it now that from our eyes
The bitter tear drops fall? We sit and weep
In humble homes : we feel a sad surprise
That death could wrest our hero from our keep
And our rich vintage reap.

Whom battle scathe avoided in the rush
Of war's loud clamors round his naked head—
Whom treason could not slay, nor terrors crush,
Of him thruout the land he saved, 'tis said
That Grant is dead.

A nation helpless at an open grave!
'Tis God's last quickening crucible to prove him.
Of all we longed to do could only love him—
And close the stone-sealed sepulchre above him.

Now lift, O Citizen, thy hands to heaven
And swear thy children's heritage shall be
Purged from the old disloyal, hateful leaven.
A land united, virtuous and free
From sea to sea.

The king is dead. There is no heir to claim
The mantle of his greatness. We must own
There is no breathing man, nor buried fame
Worthy to sit upon the vacant throne—
Forever his—alone!

The School at Talladega

Backward thro' slow decades to run
'Neath Alabama's burning sun
A building grew; from sill to roof
Its joints and planks and timbers proof.
No shams the sturdy workmen gave,
The master builder was a slave.
Of stately mold, with deft right hand
His fertile brain the structure planned.
He knew each use and staunch and fair
Framed pupil's desk and teacher's chair—
Till room by room it grew complete,
A schoolhouse shrine for youthful feet.

Oft as he toiled he thought: "Alas,
No child of mine can ever pass
Thro' these fair portals; no blest draught
Of learning from this fount be quaffed.
I build the temple—but the fire
Its altar warms no son nor sire
Of my sad race can ever know
The rapture of its fervent glow.
Books are the master's heritage,
The slave reads not the printed page."

Musing he slept and dreamed a dream—
He heard the blaring trumpet's scream
The bugle note—the clamorous drum
Of bannered hosts the warlike hum;
There wandered o'er his wildered ken
Blood, battles, groans of wounded men—
And wheeling squadrons charging down
And death shells hurtling thro' the town.

Amid the warrior hosts in blue
He thought the Savior's face he knew;
He spake, "Oh, son, lift up thine head,
And take thy country's flag!" he said.
"Stars are the meeds that victor's please;
Thy body hath borne stripes; bear these.
Forever more thou shalt be free!
Not judgment this—but jubilee!"

He took the flag, and in the front
Of many a bitter battle's brunt
He wrapped its folds his body round,
Nor suffered it to touch the ground—
Till victory swept from sea to sea,
The land was saved—the slave was free.

His dream went on; he saw the sky
Clear brightly as the clouds rolled by;
He saw once more that old school house
Beneath its shade of piny boughs,
A hum of voices filled the place,
And lo! the children of his race.
Dusk groups of freedmen's sons and daughters
Drank from this fountain wisdom's waters.
Children of his own blood were there.
In transports of a happy prayer
Of thanks to God he woke. But you
Know that the poor slave's dream came true.

Mabel

What, make a poem of our household pet?
    She is a poem ready made, you know;
A piece of God's fair handiwork—just let
    To brighten, for a space, our home below.

There's naught on earth that seemeth half so fair
    To my fond eyes—so perfect and complete—
From the soft ripplings of her gold-brown hair
    Down to the dimples in her tiny feet.

The starry brightness of her winsome eyes,
    The snowy lids with dusky fringes hung,
Her cunning household pranks—her sweet replies—
    The liquid music of her lisping tongue.

The sweet red lips with kisses brimming o'er
    And loving words for every living thing—
Her pearly teeth—in number just a score—
    Heart treasures all, to me; with power to bring

Back from the vanished past the olden days
    And lighten every burden of the hour
With dreams that fill the future's misty haze
    As golden buds bespeak the coming flower.

Three shining linklets in her chain of years
    Are finished; polished fair each silver strand.
The length of that dear chain not yet appears,
    Its clasps are hidden in the Father's hand.

Just entering the valley, green and fair—
    What hills and darksome mountains lie before
We know not; but we'll shield her with a prayer;
    God guide her safely to the golden door!

A Garden Ballad

Sweet William wooed fair Marigold;
Sweet William wore a Prince's feather
No Cockscomb he—a soldier bold,
With Larkspurs on his patent leather.

Upon his hands Foxgloves so Spruce—
His steed he urged—nor stayed, nor tarried
A silken snow White-flag of truce
Upon a Golden Rod he carried.

No Monk's Hood capped him from the sky
With wreath of Maiden's Hair—bespoken—
He wore upon his helmet high
His Lady's Slipper for a token.

A maiden fair was Marigold,
Her Virgin's Bower in gardens shady
With faithful servitors in hold
An Old man and a Ragged lady.

Her Colt's Foot pawed the Meadowsweet
Her Phlox were tended leal and loyal,
Her Shepherd's purse was still replete
With Moneyvine and Pennyroyal.

But sore she mourned her absent love,
With Canterbury Bells Sloe chiming,
Her Blueflag furled on tower above,
Her sad thoughts to a sad tune rhyming.

My-Love-lies-Bleeding," oft she cried—
"While Nightshades dim my Morning Glory;
And I must Pine a Mourning-bride
Where Windflowers chant my fateful story."

Sometimes she smiled in hopeful part—
"O, my Sweet William! Live-for-ever!
Bring Balm to heal my Bleeding Heart.
Forget-me-not! Forget me never!"

The clouds are clearing from her sky,
The Catch-flies to the breeze are humming,
She sees her lover drawing nigh,
Her Thyme has come, for he is coming. .

"My Heart's-Delight," she cried elate—
"Sure Heart's ease blooms in summer weather."
"O, Kiss-me-over-the-garden-gate,
Sweet William, with the Prince's feather."

"Orchis me with thine own Tulips,
My Bridal-rose, my sweet Spring-beauty!
Upon thy Lily finger tips
I press the Golden Seal of duty."

Bessie

Ancestress of "Hoosier Belle," "Josephine," "Little Robert Dillon,"
"Jack" and "Tom"

With an eye like a hawk, and a head like a fawn,
And slim, jetty legs—swift as lances of dawn—
So gentle, so fearless, so ready to do,
So gallant in bearing, in spirit so true.
Now who is this faithfullest, prettiest horse?
Why, Bessie, of course.

We love her, and pat her, and stroke her, nor miss
The kind pretty nose she holds out for a kiss;
We call her pet names: "Sweetheart," "Lady" and "Dear
And watch the soft, quivering, sensitive ear,
As she listens; this knowing, intelligent horse!
Is Bessie, of course.

Black, red, roan or dappled, white, sorrel or gray,
Cream-colored, brown, chestnut, or claybank, or bay,
Stand all together in gallant array.
Look them well over, and tell me, I pray,
Which is the darlingest, cunningest horse?
Why, Bessie, of course!

Hoosier Belle

On a gala day the crowd
Musters equipages proud—
Glancing hoof and harness sheen;
But of all the steeds that meet
Thronging down the stately street,
Stepping slowly, stepping fleet,
La Belle Hoosier is the queen.

Hoosier with her deer-like head,
And her dainty feet that tread
Lightly, proudly on the way;
With her silken, shining coat,
Love locks tossing, mane a-float,
And her human, whinnied note
When she smells the clover hay.

Vainly on the freshening wind
Come the hoof-beats close behind
With their rhythmic ebb and swell,
Thou and I, dear, have no need
Of the fabled wing-ed steed,
When we put her to her speed—
Bonnie little Hoosier Belle!

Josephine

Bring no silken reins to me,
Till my lady's face I see;
Golden bits I will refuse
Till my lady dear shall choose.
O, her hands, so velvet fine!
O, her eyes, that look in mine!
O, her voice, so sweet, so dear!
When she whispers in my ear;
Yes, she whispers—while I lean
Close to hear her—"Josephine,"
"Best of horses, stable queen!
"Josephine!"

All the world shall see and hear
How I love my lady dear.
All the world shall hear and see
How my lady dear loves me!
O, for her I grandly toss
All this wealth of ebon floss;
Show my proudest, fleetest pace
For the love of her dear face;
For the love-touch of her hand's
Welcome gesture of command.
Lightest step and loftiest mien,
When she calls me—"Josephine"—
I'm her darling, stable queen—
Josephine.

Little Robert Dillon

Heard of Hoosier Belle and Bessie?
Finest horses in the land,
With one notable exception, which I was
        about to make,
That's me—Little Robert Dillon—
One of Bessie's gay grandchildren,
And I'm told I "take the cake."

Hoosier Belle's my pretty mother,
And I look just like her—so!
As one pea is like another—
Only swifter on the go.
Only neater, sweeter, fleeter,
As a darling pet, completer—
And I should be—for her sake.
For I'm little Robert Dillon,
One of Bessie's gay grandchildren,
And I think I take the cake.

O'er a better back than mine,
Never hope to draw a line,
Not a bit of use to try it;
Take a ribbon blue and tie it
To my headstall; tie it higher
As befits a gallant flyer;
And to me obeisance make,
For I'm Little Robert Dillon,
One of Bessie's gay grandchildren,
And I know I take the cake.

At Snoqualmie Falls

I have seen thy hills, Snoqualmie,
Silver-hooded through the mist—
Temples veiled in solemn splendor,
Bases swathed in amethyst.

When God set the granite mountains
At the dawning of creation,
Did some worshipful, strong angel
Pour thee out as a libation?

Did he fling thee down, Snoqualmie,
From the purple of thy hills—
Gathering for thy leaping billows
Waters of a thousand rills?

Oh, thou silver-throated wonder!
Lonely falls of mystery!
Wert thou poured out for the mountains—
Or the mountains framed for thee?

A Symphony

Athwart gray waves the vessels go,
Mid soft gray skies the sun hangs low.

The sea gulls skim and float and dip
Their long gray wings beside the ship.

In mists the far horizons die—
Vague blendings of the sea and sky.

But look! the sun sends down to me
A golden path across the sea.

Opportunity

On his own affairs attent—
Passing near the city gate,
Where the Christ a-weary bent
Neath the heavy timber's weight—
Midst the riot, rush and cry,
When the haughty Roman's eye
Fell on this stout passer-by.

Simon of Cyrene, Oh, say!
When on thee they laid the cross
Didst thou curse—or bless the day—
Count it gain, or grievous loss?
Simon, Simon! didst thou know
All the glory of that woe—
Joy of joys to serve Him so?

Dead and buried thou hast been
Twice a thousand years; and yet
Simon—Simon of Cyrene!
All too short for sore regret—
All too recent to forget—
If the cross when laid on thee
Was upborne unwillingly.

Sue, at Nineteen

There were violets in the hollow of the wood
And beneath the sodden leafage of the vale,
Where our ancient, towering beech and maples stood,
And the early springtime flowers never fail.

And the violets were heaven's own blue,
O, we plucked them, neath the sweet May skies,
And the velvet petals wore the very hue
That I used to see—my sister—in thine eyes.

There were roses in the thickets growing wild,
Mid a tangle of sweet briar blooming fair,
Like thy cheeks they were—those roses undefiled—
In the tangle of thy dusky, silken hair.

There were happy birds that sang among the trees,
And the brook beyond our wheat fields rippled low,
And the music of the merriest of these
Is thy voice as I recall it, long ago.

Puget Sound at Night

Gray-tissued veils of mist threads interwoven
    Shrouds all our daylight world—our vision bars,
But one sweet night I looked up into heaven
    And saw the blessed stars.

The blessed, friendly stars! In calm content
    Thro far, dim spaces, move so white and high—
They are the gifts of Love: for comfort meant
    As the slow dark goes by.

I cannot deem them worlds like unto this,
    With ebb and flow of pulsing water's tide,
And human hearts a-throbbing woe and bliss,
    Where human homes abide.

Remote they shine: their radiances blent
    In stately harmonies covet not release—
We cannot fret them with our discontent,
    Vex with our wars their peace.

Tho mute, they are not inarticulate,
    Save as our dullness their great message mars:
He only wins his soul's complete estate
    Who looks beyond the stars.

After Appomattox

We walked beneath the orchard trees,
    The July sun shone in its prime—
The ruddy clovers swept our knees;
    That happy summer time.

The mother's face was glorified,
    For all the thunders of the guns
Were hushed, and when the echoes died
    She welcomed home her sons.

They looked upon us as men look
    Who greet their kin in paradise;
And we—our souls with gladness shook,
    Our very hearts were in our eyes.

Forgetting pain and mortal strife,
    They laughed with us beneath the trees—
They were our dead come back to life,
    The heroes of the hard-won peace.

We listened to the tales they told,
    We touched with awe the chevrons' hem;
We loved them with a love four-fold—
    Their flag—their dangers—service—them.

They loved not strife, nor war nor wound—
 But we—for their sakes cherished sword and gun—
The garb they wore—the very ground
 Their patriot feet had trod upon.

Holy their cause and righteous seemed
 The nation's life to oneness drew;
They were returned with pledge redeemed,
 And not one star lost from the blue,

So Righteousness and Mercy kissed,
 And thus the country's peace was won—
But many a soldier's mother missed
 Her unreturning son.

CPSIA information can be obtained
at www.ICGtesting.com
Printed in the USA
BVHW031142021118
531990BV00020B/1292/P

9 781331 554059